W9-DDB-301

SUDAN

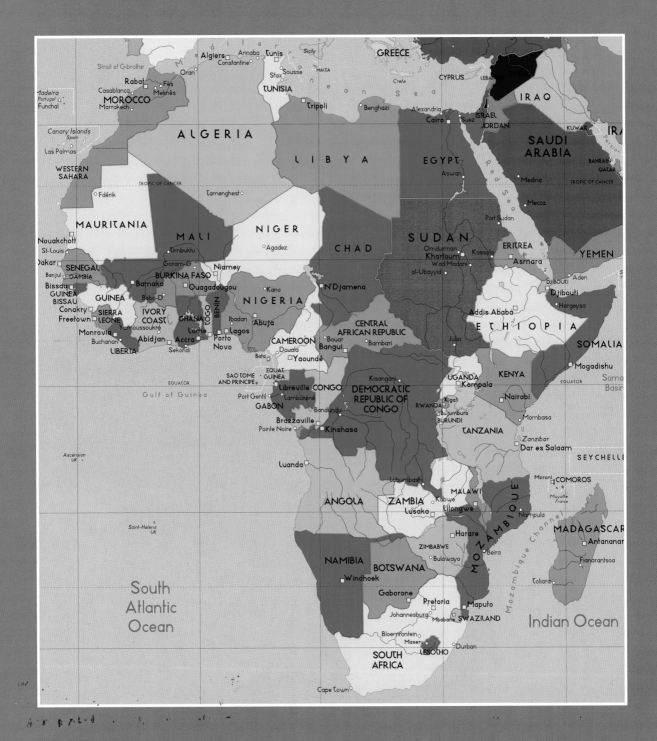

SUDAN

Dorothy Kavanaugh

Mason Crest Publishers
Philadelphia

Produced by OTTN Publishing, Stockton, N.J.

Mason Crest Publishers
370 Reed Road
Broomall, PA 19008
www.masoncrest.com

First printing

1 3 5 7 9 8 6 4 2

Library of Congress Cataloging-in-Publication Data

Kavanaugh, Dorothy, 1969-
  Sudan / Dorothy Kavanaugh.
      p. cm. — (Africa)
  Includes bibliographical references and index.
  ISBN-13: 978-1-4222-0085-8
  ISBN-10: 1-4222-0085-X
  1. Sudan. I. Title. II. Series: Africa (Philadelphia, Pa.)
  DT154.6.K384 2007
  962.4—dc22

                                            2006017641

Africa: Facts and Figures	**Egypt**	**Nigeria**
The African Union	**Ethiopia**	**Rwanda**
Algeria	**Ghana**	**Senegal**
Angola	**Ivory Coast**	**Sierra Leone**
Botswana	**Kenya**	**South Africa**
Burundi	**Liberia**	**Sudan**
Cameroon	**Libya**	**Tanzania**
Democratic Republic	**Morocco**	**Uganda**
of the Congo	**Mozambique**	**Zimbabwe**

Table of Contents

Africa: Continent in the Balance
Robert I. Rotberg

Africa is the cradle of humankind, but for millennia it was off the familiar, beaten path of global commerce and discovery. Its many peoples therefore developed largely apart from the diffusion of modern knowledge and the spread of technological innovation until the 17th through 19th centuries. With the coming to Africa of the book, the wheel, the hoe, and the modern rifle and cannon, foreigners also brought the vastly destructive transatlantic slave trade, oppression, discrimination, and onerous colonial rule. Emerging from that crucible of European rule, Africans created nationalistic movements and then claimed their numerous national independences in the 1960s. The result is the world's largest continental assembly of new countries.

There are 53 members of the African Union, a regional political grouping, and 48 of those nations lie south of the Sahara. Fifteen of them, including mighty Ethiopia, are landlocked, making international trade and economic growth that much more arduous and expensive. Access to navigable rivers is limited, natural harbors are few, soils are poor and thin, several countries largely consist of miles and miles of sand, and tropical diseases have sapped the strength and productivity of innumerable millions. Being landlocked, having few resources (although countries along Africa's west coast have tapped into deep offshore petroleum and gas reservoirs), and being beset by malaria, tuberculosis, schistosomiasis, AIDS, and many other maladies has kept much of Africa poor for centuries.

Thirty-five of the world's 50 poorest countries are African. Hunger is common. So is rapid deforestation and desertification. Unemployment rates are often over 50 percent, for jobs are few—even in agriculture. Where Africa once was a land of small villages and a few large cities, with almost everyone

Sudan is the largest country in Africa, covering an area of 967,494 square miles (2,505,810 square kilometers). It is roughly one-fourth the size of the United States.

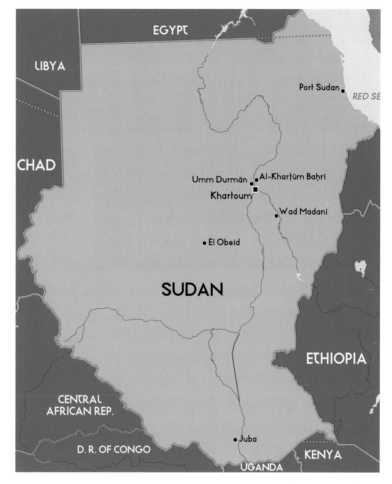

engaged in growing grain or root crops or grazing cattle, camels, sheep, and goats, today more than half of all the more than 900 million Africans, especially those who live south of the Sahara, reside in towns and cities. Traditional agriculture hardly pays, and a number of countries in Africa—particularly the smaller and more fragile ones—can no longer feed themselves.

There is not one Africa, for the continent is full of contradictions and variety. Of the 750 million people living south of the Sahara, at least 130 million live in Nigeria, 74 million in Ethiopia, 62 million in the Democratic Republic of the

Women carry water from an irrigation canal back to their village in central Sudan.

Congo, and 44 million in South Africa. By contrast, tiny Djibouti and Equatorial Guinea have fewer than 1 million people each, and prosperous Botswana and Namibia each are under 2.5 million in population. Within some countries, even medium-sized ones like Zambia (11.5 million), there are a plethora of distinct ethnic groups speaking separate languages. Zambia, typical with its multitude of competing entities, has 70 such peoples, roughly broken down into four language and cultural zones. Three of those languages jostle with English for primacy.

Given the kaleidoscopic quality of African culture and deep-grained poverty, it is no wonder that Africa has developed economically and politically less rapidly than other regions. Since independence from colonial rule, weak governance has also plagued Africa and contributed significantly to the widespread poverty of its peoples. Only Botswana and offshore Mauritius have been governed democratically without interruption since independence. Both are among Africa's wealthiest countries, too, thanks to the steady application of good governance.

Aside from those two nations, and South Africa, Africa has been a continent of coups since 1960, with massive and oil-rich Nigeria suffering incessant periods of harsh, corrupt, autocratic military rule. Nearly every other country on or around the continent, small and large, has been plagued by similar bouts of instability and dictatorial rule. In the 1970s and 1980s Idi Amin ruled Uganda capriciously and Jean-Bedel Bokassa proclaimed himself emperor of the Central African Republic. Macias Nguema of Equatorial Guinea was another in that same mold. More recently Daniel arap Moi held Kenya in thrall and Robert Mugabe has imposed himself on once-prosperous Zimbabwe. In both of those cases, as in the case of the late Gnassingbe Eyadema in Togo and Mobutu Sese Seko in Congo, these presidents stole wildly and drove entire peoples and their nations into penury. Corruption is common in Africa, and so are weak rule-of-law frameworks, misplaced development, high expenditures on soldiers and low expenditures on health and education, and a widespread (but not universal) refusal on the part of leaders to work well for their followers and citizens.

Conflict between groups within countries has also been common in Africa. More than 15 million Africans have been killed in the civil wars of Africa since 1990, with more than 3 million losing their lives in Congo and more than 2 million in the Sudan. Since 2003, according to the United Nations, more than 200,000 people have been killed in an ethnic-cleansing rampage in Sudan's Darfur region. In 2007, major civil wars and other serious conflicts persisted in Burundi, the Central African Republic, Chad, the Democratic Republic of the Congo, Ivory Coast, Sudan (in addition to the mayhem in Darfur), Uganda, and Zimbabwe.

Despite such dangers, despotism, and decay, Africa is improving. Botswana and Mauritius, now joined by South Africa, Senegal, and Ghana, are beacons of democratic growth and enlightened rule. Uganda and Senegal are taking the lead in combating and reducing the spread of AIDS, and others are following. There are serious signs of the kinds of progressive economic policy changes that might lead to prosperity for more of Africa's peoples. The trajectory in Africa is positive.

Fertile land, desert, grasslands, and swamp can all be found in Sudan. (Opposite) Lush vegetation grows along the banks of the Nile River in Sudan. (Right) Some Sudanese still use camels for transportation across the country's desert.

1 The Land and Climate

AHLAN WA SAHLAN! That's how residents of northern Sudan might greet a visitor to their country, using an Arabic phrase that means "welcome, make yourself at home." Arabic is the official language of Sudan, a country located in northern Africa, south of Egypt. Sudan's other neighbors include Libya to the northwest, Chad and the Central African Republic to the west, the Democratic Republic of the Congo, Uganda, and Kenya to the south, and Ethiopia and Eritrea to the east.

Sudan is the largest country in Africa in total area and the ninth largest in the world. The country includes nearly a million square miles (2.5 million square kilometers) of varied terrain: desert, *savanna*, rainforest, and swamp. Unfortunately, this vast country has been devastated by more than a half-century of conflict, most recently in the Darfur region of western Sudan.

A Variety of Climates

The heat in Sudan can be oppressive. Sudan is located north of the equator, in a region known as the Torrid Zone. This area is between the Tropic of Cancer in the northern hemisphere and the Tropic of Capricorn in the southern hemisphere. The Torrid Zone receives more direct sunlight than any other part of the earth.

Because Sudan is located in the tropics, temperatures are hot all year long. In the capital city of Khartoum, where most of the country's population is clustered, temperatures often surpass 100° Fahrenheit (38° Celsius) during the summer. The high humidity in the city makes the heat even harder to bear. Temperatures in the desert can climb to 110°F (43°C) in the summer, although on a winter night they may drop as low as 40°F (4°C). The southern portion of the country, which gets the most rainfall, has an average annual temperature of 86°F (30°C).

Annual rainfall in desert regions of Sudan, which are mainly in the north and west, can be as little as 0.08 inches (0.2 centimeters). Direct sunlight and hot winds have dried out the soil in Sudan's desert areas, making it incapable of trapping the little rainfall that occurs, so virtually nothing can grow. More precipitation falls to the south. The central part of the country receives about 16 inches (40 cm) of rain a year, while southern Sudan receives about 40 inches (100 cm) of rain a year.

For most of the country the rainy season occurs between April and October, although in the far south precipitation is common all year long. The increased rainfall during the summer months occurs in part because

Quick Facts: The Geography of Sudan

Location: Northern Africa, bordering the Red Sea, between Egypt and Eritrea

Area: (slightly more than one-fourth the size of the United States)
- *total:* 967,494 square miles (2,505,810 sq km)
- *land:* 917,378 square miles (2,376,000 sq km)
- *water:* 50,120 square miles (129,810 sq km)

Borders: Central African Republic, 724 miles (1,165 km); Chad 845 miles (1,360 km); Democratic Republic of the Congo, 390 miles (628 km); Egypt, 791 miles (1,273 km); Eritrea, 376 miles (605 km); Ethiopia, 998 miles (1,606 km); Kenya, 144 miles (232 km); Libya, 238 miles (383 km); Uganda, 270 miles (435 km); coastline, 530 miles (853 km)

Climate: tropical in south; arid desert in north; rainy season varies by region (April to October)

Terrain: generally flat, featureless plain; mountains in east and west; desert dominates the north

Elevation extremes:
- *lowest point:* Red Sea 0 feet (0 meters)
- *highest point:* Kinyeti 10,456 feet (3,187 meters)

Natural hazards: dust storms and periodic persistent droughts

Source: CIA World Factbook, 2007.

moisture-laden winds blow in from the Congo River Basin to the south. However, if these winds are late in developing, drought and famine can occur. This happens periodically, most recently in 2004 and 2005.

Another climate problem in Sudan is the occurrence of dust storms known as *haboobs*. These are caused by strong winds that originate to the north, in the Sahara Desert of Libya and Egypt. During these storms, which typically sweep across central Sudan between May and July, a wall of dust may totally block out the sun. *Haboobs* can last three or four days, making

This satellite photo shows an enormous dust storm blowing out of Sudan across the Red Sea.

travel impossible. Sudan is one of the few countries in the world that experiences these storms.

Geographic Regions and Features

About 25 percent of Sudan, mostly in the north, is desert. Both the Libyan desert in the northwest and the Nubian desert in the north-central part of the country are harsh places where sand dunes and scorpions are plentiful, but rain and vegetation are rare. Elsewhere, Sudan is composed of savanna, green jungles, and forests. About 19 percent of the country is forest and woodland, while about 46 percent of the country is permanent pastureland. Only a small amount of this land is used for growing crops; the rest is used for grazing herds.

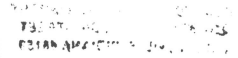

Water is precious in the northern and western parts of the country. In northern Sudan rich soil can only be found in a small strip of land along the Nile River. In western Sudan, where there are no permanent streams or large bodies of fresh water, people and animals cannot venture far from wells or waterholes. In southern Sudan, where rain is more common, the soil is quite fertile. However, farming in the country is hampered by periodic droughts as well as soil erosion.

Although the terrain in Sudan is mostly flat, the country does have several mountain ranges. The Red Sea Hills overlook the Red Sea in the east, while the Marra Mountains tower over Darfur in the western part of the country. In the southeast, visitors can find the Didinga Hills, Dongotona Mountains, and the Imatong Mountains. The Nuba Mountains in central Sudan house fertile valleys where cotton and *sorghum* are farmed.

The Nile and The Sudd

The Nile is the world's longest river, traveling some 3,470 miles (5,584 kilometers) from Lake Victoria in East Africa through Sudan to Egypt in North Africa. A small riverboat making the trip might need as long as eight days to travel the 1,200 miles (1,900 km) from the spot where the river enters Sudan in the south to the border with Egypt in the north. As the Nile flows through the eastern part of the country, it provides drinking water for people and animals, a home for fish, a source of electricity, and—when its annual summer flood arrives—rich sediment for growing crops.

The Nile is actually two rivers: the Blue Nile, which flows across Sudan from Ethiopia, and the White Nile, which enters Sudan from Uganda. The

White Nile is the longer and calmer of the two, but the Blue Nile provides a greater volume of water when the two rivers come together near Khartoum. The two rivers are named for the color of their water, although the White Nile actually appears more muddy gray than white. If one stands at the Blue Nile at dawn or dusk its water will appear very blue.

The White Nile's source is Lake Victoria in Uganda, Tanzania, and Kenya, some 2,000 miles (3,218 km) from the point where the two Niles come together. In Sudan the river first passes through an enormous swampland called the Sudd. The Sudd (this name comes from the Arabic word *sadd*, meaning "barrier") covers 6,370 square miles (16,492 sq km) during the country's dry season. During the wet summers, it can expand to cover as much as 12,350 square miles (31,974 sq km), an area the size of the state of Maryland. This enormous marsh area contains dense thickets of papyrus and other plants. At times the vegetation is so thick that the river seems to disappear.

Flora and Fauna of Sudan

The typical wildlife of Sudan includes elephants, monkeys, and tropical birds, which live in the southern forests and jungles, while crocodiles and hippos live in the rivers. The grasslands are home to giraffes, lions, cheetahs, zebras, antelope, rhinoceros, and leopards. The Sudd is frequented by crocodiles, hippos, and other animals, as well as countless species of tropical insects.

Little vegetation is found in the northern desert areas; the substantial forests are found in central and southern Sudan. Savanna-type elephant grass covers much of the central *steppe* region. The river valleys are home to a wide

An aerial view of the Sudd swamp in southern Sudan. The swampland grows significantly during the rainy season, and crocodiles and hippopotami are among the many animals that live in its shallow waters.

variety of trees, such as acacia, ebony, and baobab. Cotton, papyrus, rubber, and castor-oil plants are also *indigenous* to the Nile Basin. Animals that live in the southern region include gazelles, zebras, antelopes, and black rhinoceros.

Sudan has been torn by civil strife for decades. (Opposite) The ongoing conflict in Darfur has drawn world attention. This photo was taken at a 2006 "Save Darfur" rally in Washington, D.C. (Right) Jaafar al-Nimeri's decision to impose Islamic law on Sudan in 1983 caused leaders in southern Sudan to restart a civil war.

2 The History of Sudan

Modern Sudan is a divided land—the Arab and Muslim culture of the north is very different from the tribal culture of the south. Tragically, the differences between these two cultures have led to almost constant conflict since the country became independent in 1956. In recent years the two sides have agreed to work together and reunite the country; however, suspicion and mistrust on both sides have slowed progress toward peace and unity.

Ancient History

Human history in the area of present-day Sudan dates back thousands of years. Ancient Egyptian traders followed the Nile River south into the region, which they called Kush, around 2000 B.C. When they arrived, they found a people called the Nubians who lived along the Nile. The Nubians were farmers, herdsmen, and hunters.

Around the year 1550 B.C., the armies of the Egyptian Pharaoh Ahmose I invaded Kush, conquering the region and making it a province of Egypt. However, Kush eventually grew stronger than Egypt. In the eleventh century B.C. a Nubian society based at the city of Napata regained independence from Egyptian rule. By the eighth century, the Nubians had conquered part of southern Egypt and established the powerful Kingdom of Kush.

The Nubians eventually moved their capital to Meroe, a city on the Nile just north of present-day Khartoum. Meroe's culture was similar to Egypt's in many ways. Pottery and burial *talismans* have been found in Sudan that are older than similar discoveries made in Egypt. This indicates that both civilizations influenced the other. The Nubians built burial pyramids for their rulers; although they are much smaller than the enormous pyramids of Egypt, there are more of them. At one time, the two civilizations had similar languages and religions, but over time these became very different.

Although the Nubians were forced out of Egypt around 670 B.C., the Merotic civilization flourished until the first century B.C. After the Roman Empire conquered Egypt in 30 B.C., a Roman army invaded northern Sudan to stop Nubian raids into Egypt. In 23 B.C., the Romans sacked Meroe, sending the kingdom into a period of decline. About A.D. 350, Meroe was invaded and completely destroyed by the Axumites, a tribe from modern Ethiopia.

The Romans continued to exert a strong influence over the Sudan region for several hundred years. However, Rome itself went into a period of decline during the fourth and fifth centuries. The empire was divided into western and eastern halves after 395. After Rome, the capital of the eastern empire, fell to barbarians in 476, the eastern (or Byzantine) empire maintained control

The ancient civilizations of Meroe and Egypt shared many characteristics. For example, the people of Meroe buried their rulers in pyramids like this one.

over Egypt. However, the Byzantines did not have the resources to project their military power south into Nubia. Tribal groups stepped in to fill the power vacuum.

The Arrival of Islam

By the sixth century, three new kingdoms had emerged in the Sudan region along the Nile: Nobatia, Muqurra, and Alwa. Christianity was the official religion of each state, but each kingdom adhered to a different *sect*. This led to occasional fighting.

By the seventh century, the Africans faced a new enemy. Arab tribes, united by the Prophet Muhammad's new religion, Islam, emerged from the Arabian Peninsula after Muhammad's death in 632. They spread their religion by conquering neighboring territories, such as Persia and Egypt. Perhaps in response to this threat, Nobatia and Muqurra merged into a new, stronger state, the kingdom of Dunqulah.

The Nubians of Dunqulah were able to defeat an Arab army in 652. This led to a peace agreement, known as the *bakt*, which lasted for centuries. Under the *bakt*, the Nubians sent hundreds of slaves to Egypt each year in exchange for food and other goods. Arab language and customs gradually took root, particularly in the north, because the Nubians had to learn Arabic in order to trade with their neighbors. Islam spread gradually through the spread of Arab settlers and Muslim missionaries.

Dunqulah grew weaker after the tenth century. In 1276 the Mamluks, a powerful group of Muslims who ruled Egypt, helped overthrow the king of Dunqulah and placed a new king on the throne. Though Dunqulah remained nominally independent, the Mamluks essentially controlled the state. As Muslims gained power in the region, the Nubian Christian church declined. In 1315 the first Muslim king of Dunqulah took the throne, and by 1500 most people of Dunqulah had converted to Islam. In 1517 the powerful Ottoman Empire absorbed both Egypt and Dunqulah.

To the south, the kingdom of Alwa was also on the decline. Around 1500, the kingdom fell to the Funj, a race of black Africans who practiced Islam.

The Funj would continue to rule the southern region until the 19th century. In east Sudan, another small Funj kingdom arose—the kingdom of Sennar, which thrived from the 16th to the 18th centuries.

Foreign Involvement

By the end of the 18th century, most of Sudan was considered part of Egypt, and thus under Ottoman control. However, European countries were growing interested in North Africa. In 1798, a French army led by Napoleon Bonaparte invaded Egypt. Although the Ottomans, with the help of Great Britain, forced the French to leave in 1801, the region entered a chaotic period.

In 1805, the Ottoman sultan appointed a man named Muhammad Ali to rule Egypt. Once Ali had gained control over the country, he decided to make Egypt independent of the Ottoman Empire. To do this, he would need money and a strong military. In 1820 Ali's forces invaded Sudan, where he hoped to acquire gold and slaves to serve in his army. Within a year, 50,000 Sudanese had been killed and another 30,000 sent north to Egypt as slaves.

The Egyptian invasion marked the start of 60 years of Egyptian rule over Sudan. The

The Egyptian ruler Muhammad Ali invaded Sudan in 1820 and soon brought the region under his control.

Egyptians were harsh rulers. They extracted high taxes and exploited or enslaved the nomadic people of the region. However, under Egyptian rule modern farming and irrigation techniques were introduced, and railroad and telegraph lines were constructed.

Europeans remained interested in Egypt and its Sudan territory. In the 1850s a French company began working on a canal that would connect the Mediterranean Sea with the Red Sea and Indian Ocean. The Suez Canal opened in 1869. For Great Britain, the canal was an important connection to its colony in India. To protect this connection the British became more involved in Egyptian affairs. In 1882 the British took control of Egypt's government, although nominally the country remained part of the Ottoman Empire.

The Mahdi's Rebellion

In Sudan, a charismatic Muslim leader named Muhammad Ahmed soon rebelled against British rule. Ahmed was a leader of a fringe Islamic sect called Sammaniyah; he claimed to be the Mahdi, a prophet sent to prepare Muslims for the end of the world. In 1883, the Mahdi called for a holy war (or *jihad*) against Sudan's Egyptian and British occupiers. He achieved a series of impressive military victories, including the defeat of 7,000 Egyptian troops near al-Ubayyid and the massacre of British troops under General Charles Gordon after the 1884–85 siege of Khartoum. After these defeats, the British and Egyptians withdrew from Sudan.

The Mahdi died just five months after the victory at Khartoum. Although he set up a government before he died, over the next few years Sudan became a chaotic place as various leaders fought for power. In 1891,

Abdullah ibn Muhammad emerged from the fighting as *khalifa*, or ruler, of Sudan. However, this did not stabilize the country. According to some sources, about half of the population died due to famine, disease, persecution, and warfare between 1885 and 1900.

During the mid-1890s, the British government decided to regain control over Sudan. The major battle occurred at Omdurman, a small city just north of Khartoum where the Mahdi's tomb was located. Although the British were heavily outnumbered, they were armed with machine guns and modern artillery. This turned the battle in their favor; British casualties were 48 dead and 382 wounded, compared to some 10,000 dead, 15,000 wounded, and 5,000 captured on the Sudanese side.

With the *khalifa* defeated, British leaders established the modern borders of Sudan. These borders included two distinctly different regions. Most of the people who lived in northern Sudan were Muslims of Arab descent. Culturally, they were similar to the people of Egypt and other Arab countries. The people of southern Sudan were black African tribesmen, most of whom were Christians or animists. Culturally, they were more like the people of other sub-Saharan African countries. The cultural and religious differences would create tension between the two areas of the country.

The Condominium Period

In 1899 Britain and Egypt agreed to share control of Sudan. Their agreement, called the **condominium**, brought about a relatively prosperous and peaceful period for Sudan. However, decisions made during this time would sow the

Britain's long rule in Sudan (1899–1956) is evident in this photograph of Khartoum, taken around 1936. The statue depicts Herbert Horatio Kitchener, the British general who defeated the Sudanese army at the Battle of Omdurman in 1898.

seeds of eventual discord. The British rulers treated the northern and southern areas of the country differently. They modernized northern Sudan, where most of the people lived, expanding telegraph and rail services and helping farmers grow cotton and other cash crops for export. At the same time, believing that the south was not ready for modernization, the British issued laws that prohibited outsiders from working or traveling there. The British discouraged the black African tribesmen from adopting Islam, speaking

Arabic, or dressing like their northern countrymen. Instead they encouraged the spread of Christianity and allowed Christian missionaries to enter the area and establish churches and schools. The British also permitted greater tribal autonomy in the south than in the north.

Although Sudan was generally peaceful during the condominium period, the region had its problems. After the end of World War I (1914–18), the Ottoman Empire was dissolved and its former Arab territories in the Middle East and Africa were divided among European countries like France and Great Britain. However, many Arabs wanted complete freedom from foreign control, and independence movements grew. In Sudan, groups like the White Flag League and the Umma Party urged freedom from Britain and Egypt during the 1920s and 1930s.

World War II (1939–1945) interrupted the debate on Sudanese independence, but by the late 1940s the issue emerged again. In 1948 the pro-independence Umma Party gained control of Sudan's legislative council and negotiated greater freedoms from British control. In February 1953, Egypt and Great Britain signed an agreement establishing a three-year transition period. Sudan would become independent on January 1, 1956.

Civil War Begins in Sudan

Sectional trouble started even before independence. Some Sudanese from the south, afraid Muslim Arabs would dominate the country, began waging a guerrilla war in the fall of 1955. They wanted to southern Sudan to become a separate country. This conflict, known as the First Sudanese Civil War, would continue on and off for the next 17 years.

A member of Sudan's legislative council stands to speak during a 1951 meeting. By this time, most members of the council supported independence for Sudan. Britain granted Sudan internal autonomy in 1953, and in 1956 the country officially became independent.

The civilian government elected in 1956 was soon overthrown by a military *coup* led by two generals, Ibrahim Abbud and Ahmad Abd al Wahab. By 1959, Abbud had complete control of Sudan's government. His policies toward southern Sudan fueled the growing insurgency there. Abbud's government tried to suppress the culture and religious beliefs of people in the south by imposing those of the Arab and Islamic north.

In addition to the civil war, the Abbud government faced opposition from other groups, including the Sudanese Communist Party and the United National Front. After riots by students, civil servants, and trade unionists in October 1964, Abbud dissolved the military regime and reinstituted a civilian government. The new government would operate under the transitional constitution of the 1950s. Sirr al-Khatim al-Khalifa was named prime minister, and a 15-seat parliament was chosen and charged with writing a new constitution for Sudan.

Elections were held in March 1965, but continuing unrest in the south prevented many people from voting. The newly elected government, led by Muhammad Ahmad Mahjub, cracked down on communists and the southern guerrillas. However, the government remained unstable. Disagreements over Sudan's direction forced Mahjub to resign as prime minister in July 1966. He was succeeded by Sadiq al-Mahdi, the son of the country's Islamic religious leader. When al-Mahdi's government also lost public confidence, Mahjub returned to power as prime minister. In 1969, a military dictator named Jaafar al-Nimeri seized control of the government.

Throughout the 1960s, the civil war drained the country of resources. By 1972, about 500,000 people had been killed in southern Sudan—80 percent of them civilians. Hoping to end the fighting and reunify the country, Nimeri agreed to negotiate with Joseph Lagu, the leader of the Southern Sudan Liberation Movement (SSLM), the main opposition group. After a conference at Addis Ababa, Ethiopia, the two sides reached an agreement. The Addis Ababa accords, signed in March 1972, provided for a cease-fire and gave the southern region some autonomy.

A Short-Lived Peace

The Addis Ababa accords brought a decade of relative peace to Sudan. However, during this time the popularity of Nimeri's government declined because of its corruption and incompetence. A drought and subsequent famine, as well as a weak economy, did not help matters. To gain support, Nimeri aligned with a *fundamentalist* Muslim party called the National Islamic Front (NIF). In 1983, he declared that all of Sudan would be subject to Islamic law (known as *Sharia*). Many people in the south were unwilling to accept this, and war erupted again. The conflict between the Sudanese People's Liberation Movement (SPLM) soon turned into a full-scale civil war. The SPLM's military arm, the Sudanese People's Liberation Army (SPLA), soon took control of many rural communities in southern Sudan.

Because of Sudan's many problems, Nimeri's government was overthrown by the military in 1985. A transitional government, led by Lieutenant General Abd ar Rahman Siwar adh Dhahab, was created. Siwar adh Dhahab wanted Sudan to have a democratic government and called for free elections in 1986. When the people went to the polls they returned former prime minister Sadiq al-Mahdi to power.

The Mahdi government was unable to end the civil war or solve the country's economic problems. Hoping for a breakthrough, Sadiq al-Mahdi promised to withdraw Sharia as the law of Sudan in 1989. However, on the day the law was to be changed, his government was overthrown by *Islamists*. The coup was planned by Hassan al-Turabi, the leader of the National Islamic Front, and carried out by General Omar Hassan al-Bashir, who became president.

Bashir declared *martial law*. He banned political parties and labor unions and reinstituted harsh Sharia punishments. By 1990 the National Congress Party, a political arm of the National Islamic Front, had gained significant power in Sudan's parliament. In 1990–91, Turabi formed an organization for

The leader of Sudan's Islamists, Hassan al-Turabi (left), engineered a 1989 coup that brought General Omar al-Bashir (right) to power. However, the onetime allies became political enemies after Turabi was elected speaker of Sudan's assembly in 1996.

militants, the Popular Arab Islamic Conference (PAIC), which was based in Khartoum. This group opposed the 1991 Gulf War against Iraq, and allowed anti-western Islamists to operate freely in Sudan. The most notorious example is Osama bin Laden, who trained terrorists in Sudan until 1996, when the U.S. pressured the Sudanese government to expel him.

In August 1998, Islamic demonstrators attacked the U.S. embassies in Kenya and Tanzania, killing 12 Americans and 300 Africans. In response, the

U.S. fired cruise missiles at the al-Shifa pharmaceutical factory in Khartoum. The CIA believed that the plant was secretly being used to manufacture nerve gas and was linked to bin Laden's terrorist organization al-Qaeda. (This claim has never been proven or disproven.)

A Break in the Fighting

Efforts to end Sudan's civil war continued through the 1990s. By 2002, the U.S. Committee for Refugees reported that more than 2 million Sudanese had died from fighting, disease, or famine since the second civil war began. Some 4 million Sudanese were displaced from their homes by the conflict, with at least 500,000 living as refugees in other countries.

In October 2002, the Sudanese government and SPLA rebels agreed to a cease-fire while representatives of the two sides met in Kenya to discuss a peaceful settlement. Peace talks continued through 2003 and 2004. On January 9, 2005, representatives of both sides signed the Naivasha Treaty. This agreement called for southern autonomy for six years. At the end of that period, the people of the South will be allowed to vote on whether they want independence, or would prefer to remain part of Sudan. In addition, all revenue from the state—particularly money from the sale of Sudan's oil and natural gas—will be shared between the northern and southern regions.

While the treaty officially ended the civil war after 21 years, there have been incidents of fighting on both sides. In addition, the Sudanese government has been condemned by the international community for its involvement in another internal war—the Darfur conflict in western Sudan.

SPLA leader John Garang (right) and Sudanese Vice President Ali Osman Taha hold up copies of the peace agreement that ended more than 20 years of civil war between the government and rebel groups in southern Sudan, January 9, 2005.

Darfur

The Darfur conflict began as a rivalry between farmers and herdsmen over pastureland. The farmers, many of whom were of African descent, attempted to prevent nomadic herdsmen of Arab ethnicity, known as the Baggara, from grazing their flocks on land used for their crops. The Baggara responded by attacking villages and forcing out the farmers.

In 2003 two groups, the Justice and Equality Movement and the Sudanese Liberation Army, rebelled against the government, claiming that it

Members of the Justice and Equality Movement (JEM), some armed with rocket-propelled grenades, gather outside a village in Darfur. Since 2003 JEM and other rebel groups have been waging a war against the Arab *janjaweed* militia, which is supported by the government.

had sided with the Baggara by assisting an Arab militia called the *janjaweed*. Both sides have been accused of significant human rights violations, including looting, rapes, mass killings, and the destruction of entire villages. In particular, the *janjaweed* has been accused of carrying out a policy of "ethnic cleansing" in the Darfur region.

The African Union brokered a ceasefire in April 2004 and sent peacekeeping troops in to ensure compliance. However, the conflict continued, and by 2006 the United Nations estimated that over 400,000 people had been killed in Darfur, with another 2 million people driven from their homes. That year the UN proposed sending a larger peacekeeping force of more than 17,000 soldiers to replace the smaller African Union force. However, Sudan refused to allow the UN peacekeepers into the country, and launched a major military offensive against the rebel groups.

Unlike Sudan's first and second civil wars, religion does not play an important part in the fighting, as most of the combatants on all sides are Muslims. Additionally, in recent years some groups of Darfuri Arabs have begun waging their own armed rebellion against the Arab government and its *janjaweed* allies, which they say do not represent them.

In early 2007, the Save Darfur Coalition announced that President al-Bashir had agreed to a cease-fire in order to work toward an agreement to end the fighting in Darfur. Despite this positive step, Sudan's future as a unified country remains uncertain. It remains to be seen whether al-Bashir and other Sudanese leaders will live up to their commitment to provide a safe and stable home for all of their country's people and end the internal fighting that has plagued this state for decades.

Despite reforms implemented as part of the 2005 peace process, Sudan remains dominated by its authoritarian president. (Opposite) Omar al-Bashir addresses the United Nations. (Right) Three leaders of Sudan's National Assembly attend a rally in Khartoum.

3 The Government of Sudan

SINCE INDEPENDENCE IN 1956, Sudan has been ruled by a succession of dictatorships and torn by civil war. In 2005 the government took steps to bring peace to Sudan by signing a power-sharing agreement with the Sudanese People's Liberation Movement, the major rebel group of southern Sudan. The two sides agreed to govern the country together for a period of six years, after which people in the south could decide through a referendum vote whether to break away and form an independent state. New elections for the president and legislature will be held in 2009, and the vote on secession is scheduled for 2010.

In the meantime, northern and southern Sudan are governed under different legal systems. In the predominantly Muslim north, laws are based on the Qur'an and the Islamic legal code Sharia, while in the south Sharia penalties are not enforced.

37

Sudan's current president, Omar al-Bashir, headed a military *junta* that took power in 1989. At the time his government had strong support from the Islamist National Congress Party (NCP), the political arm of the National Islamic Front (NIF). However, Bashir gradually moved to expand his power, and in December 1999 he dissolved Sudan's parliament over a split with NIF leader Hassan al-Turabi, the speaker of parliament and his former ally. Turabi had attempted to amend Sudan's constitution to limit the president's authority. In response Bashir took measures to preserve his rule and restrict Turabi's influence, imprisoning his rival several times.

Power in the Hands of the President

Sudan's constitution, which was adopted in 1998, gives most political power to the president. As head of government and chief of state, the president commands the military, appoints judges, and rules over a cabinet that oversees various departments of government. The president has the power to make laws and can even amend the constitution.

The presidency is an elective office, and presidents are supposed to serve five-year terms. In the most recent election, held in 2000, Bashir received more than 86 percent of the vote. However, opposition parties boycotted the election because they believed the voting was rigged in the president's favor, and most independent observers agreed the elections were neither free nor fair. The presidential elections originally planned for 2005 were rescheduled because of the peace agreement.

Under the terms of the 2005 peace agreement two vice presidents serve under the president, one from the north and one from the south. Initially,

SPLM leader John Garang was the vice president representing the south; however, after his death in a plane crash his deputy Salva Kiir Mayardit filled the position.

The president is also served by a group of ministers, each of whom oversees a government department such as agriculture, defense, or education. As part of the 2005 power-sharing agreement some ministries were allotted to the SPLM's candidates. However, Bashir's National Congress Party maintained control of several key ministries, including energy and mining, which oversees the country's lucrative oil industry. In any case the power of ministers is limited, as the president has the authority to remove them at any time.

The National Legislature

As part of the 2005 power-sharing agreement, a new parliament was created in Sudan. The National Legislature has two chambers: the National Assembly (Majlis

In 2005 Salva Kiir became the president of the autonomous government of southern Sudan, as well as one of Sudan's two vice presidents.

Watani) and the Council of States (Majlis Welayat). All members of the legislature serve six-year terms.

The National Assembly includes 450 members who are appointed by the president. Sudan's transitional constitution allotted 52 percent of the seats in the National Assembly to the National Congress Party, 28 percent to the SPLM, and the balance to other opposition groups. Under the transitional constitution, the functions of the National Assembly include monitoring the performance of the president and ministers; passing bills and laws; ratifying international treaties; and approving the annual budget.

The Council of States includes 50 members elected by the legislatures of Sudan's 26 states. The Council is responsible for overseeing relations between the states and the federal government. In addition, presidential appointments to the Constitutional Court must be approved by two-thirds of the members of the Council of States.

The president, ministers, and members of the National Legislature can all propose new laws. These are introduced into one chamber of the National Legislature, where they are reviewed and voted upon. If the law passes in one chamber, the other chamber must also pass the law before it can go into effect.

The Judicial Branch

At the top of Sudan's judicial system is a Supreme Court, which is headed by a chief justice. The Supreme Court, or Court of Cassation, is the highest level court; appeals cannot be taken any higher. However, the Supreme Court does not oversee cases concerning the constitutionality of law. Instead, a

Constitutional Court performs *judicial review*—determining whether a new law conflicts with the constitution—and hears cases concerning citizens' constitutional rights. The president appoints members of this court, but the appointments must be confirmed by the Council of States.

There are four levels of criminal and civil courts. These include Town Benches, where local matters are resolved; District Courts; Province Courts; and the Court of Appeals. This court examines cases to make sure that lower court rulings were fair and in compliance with Sudanese law.

About 80 percent of Sudan's people work in agriculture. (Opposite) A herdsman leads goats to drink in a nearby river. (Right) Farmers harvest peanuts, one of Sudan's main export crops.

4 A Struggling Economy

Sudan is a poor country with few paved roads, an inadequate water supply, a shortage of skilled labor, and little arable land. Add to the mix sectional conflicts, frequent droughts, and high *inflation* and it is easy to understand why the country's economy has suffered. The country's *gross domestic product* (GDP), a measure of the market value of all goods and services produced in the country annually, is $76 billion. Forty percent of the people in Sudan live below the poverty line.

Economic Breakdown

Agriculture is the country's greatest strength, representing 39 percent of the nation's GDP. Eighty percent of Sudanese workers make their livings farming. Cotton, peanuts, sesame seeds, and grains like sorghum, *millet*, and wheat are grown—both for use in the country and for export.

Quick Facts: The Economy of Sudan

Gross domestic product (GDP*):
$96.01 billion
Inflation: 9%
Natural resources: petroleum; small reserves of iron ore, copper, chromium ore, zinc, tungsten, mica, silver, gold, hydropower
Agriculture (35.5% of GDP): cotton, groundnuts (peanuts), sorghum, millet, wheat, gum arabic, sugarcane, cassara, mangos, papaya, bananas, sweet potatoes, sesame; sheep, livestock
Industry (24.8% of GDP): oil, cotton ginning, textiles, cement, edible oils, sugar, soap distilling, shoes, petroleum refining, pharmaceuticals, armaments, automobile/light truck assembly
Services (39.7% of GDP): government services, other

Foreign trade:
Exports–$8.7 billion: oil and petroleum products, cotton, sesame, livestock, groundnuts, gum arabic, sugar.
Imports–$7.5 billion: foodstuffs, manufactured goods, machinery and transport equipment, medicines and chemicals, textiles, wheat.
Economic growth rate: 9.6%
Currency exchange rate: U.S. $1 = 200.22 Sudanese dinars (2007)

*GDP is the total value of goods and services produced in a country annually.
All figures are 2006 estimates unless otherwise indicated.
Source: CIA World Factbook, 2007.

Sudan is the world's second-largest producer of gum arabic, a product of the acacia tree. The resin can be used to replace oil in low-fat baked goods, to thicken candies, in the adhesive on postage stamps, and to stabilize the foam in beer and soda. Before the civil war, Sudan had been the world's top producer of gum arabic but now it shares the market with the neighboring country of Chad. Chad began processing the resin at the urging of food and cosmetic industry users, who feared instability in Sudan would prevent them from obtaining this key ingredient in their products.

Industry makes up 20 percent of Sudan's GDP. This aspect of the country's economy is dominated by the processing of agricultural products, such as sugar and cotton. Cement, soap, shoe manufacturing, petroleum refining, and the manufacture of armaments and automobiles round out the list of the country's biggest industries. The government owns some industrial plants, while others are privately owned.

Service industries, from construction and plumbing to health care and professional services, constitute the remainder (about 41 percent) of Sudan's GDP.

Another large source of income for Sudan is remittances from workers elsewhere. In 2006 Sudanese citizens living and working outside of the country sent nearly a billion dollars to their families in Sudan.

The Petroleum Industry

Sudan's most promising natural resources are oil and natural gas. Experts believe the country contains 600 million to 1.2 billion barrels of oil, as well as 3 trillion cubic feet of natural gas. Although oil was discovered in 1978, the country was not able to take advantage until a pipeline from the oil fields to Port Sudan was completed in 1999. By 2002 oil generated more than $500 million in annual income for the country.

Distribution of the revenue from oil was a key element of the 2005 agreement that ended the civil war. Under the terms of the Naivasha Treaty, the autonomous southern provinces of Sudan were to share equally in the oil revenues with the government in the north.

Sudan's vice president Ali Osman Taha (second from right) watches as an engineer explains the controls at a new oil refinery.

Major oil companies from Malaysia, China, India, Sweden, Austria, France, and Canada have partnered with Sudan to extract the oil. In 2004 a Chinese company constructed a pipeline from Sudan's oil fields to a shipping terminal on the Red Sea. Currently, about 40 percent of Sudan's oil is sold to China, with Malaysia purchasing about 30 percent and India 25 percent.

In August 2006 GNPOC—a company controlled by China, Malaysia, and India—discovered a new oil field in Kordofan region. The new field currently produces 24,000 barrels a day and is expected to produce 40,000 in the future.

Imports and Exports

A trade imbalance has historically been a problem for Sudan—the country generally imported far more goods than it exported. By 2006, however, the value of Sudan's exports ($7.5 billion) nearly matched the cost of imported goods ($8.7 billion). The increase in export value mainly reflected the rising cost of oil on the world market.

Sudan's main exports include oil and petroleum products, cotton, sesame, livestock, gum arabic, and sugar. In 2006, China purchased about 70 percent ($5.3 billion) of Sudan's exports. Other major trade partners include Japan ($900 million) and Saudi Arabia ($210 million). During the 1970s Saudi Arabia invested heavily in agricultural projects in Sudan; today, the kingdom primarily purchases grain and other foodstuffs.

Commodities that Sudan imports include wheat and other foodstuffs that are not grown in the country, manufactured goods, equipment for the oil industry, medicines and chemicals, and textiles. Sudan's main import partners include China, Saudi Arabia, the United Arab Emirates, Egypt, India, Germany, Australia, and Japan.

Because of Sudan's sponsorship of terrorist groups, most U.S. companies are forbidden from doing business in Sudan. As a result the United States does relatively little trade with Sudan. According to official U.S. figures for

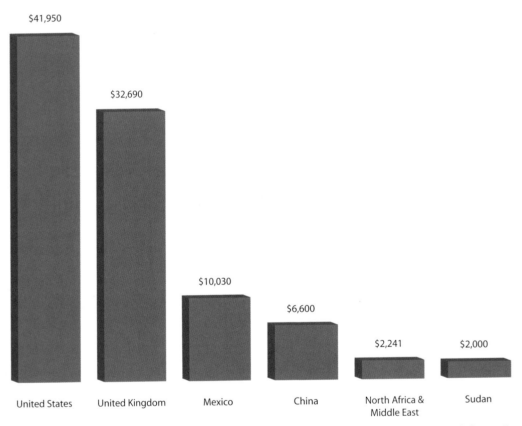

Gross National Income (GNI) Per Capita of Sudan and Other Countries*

*Gross national income per capita is the total value of all goods and services produced domestically in a year, supplemented by income received from abroad, divided by midyear population. The above figures take into account fluctuations in currency exchange rates and differences in inflation rates across global economies.

All figures are based on 2005 data. Source: World Bank, 2006.

2005, American companies sent $68 million in goods to Sudan, while Sudan exported just $3.7 million in goods to the United States.

The Future

Although Sudan's economy still has many problems, the country seems to be moving in a positive direction. Increased oil production, along with the expansion of the industrial sector, helped Sudan's GDP grow by more than 9 percent in 2006. This is a better rate of growth than many other African countries. And while the inflation rate in Sudan was estimated at 9 percent—a relatively high rate compared to Western nations like the United States—inflation is far less than it was in 1991, when the rate was 300 percent. However, if Sudan's government cannot maintain peace and political stability, most people will not feel the effects of Sudan's strengthening economy.

Many cultural and ethnic groups live in Sudan. (Opposite) A group of women pay attention to their teacher in a crudely built school near Nyala. (Right) Several of these Dinka men show distinctive scar patterns on their foreheads. The Dinka are Sudan's largest non-Muslim ethnic group, numbering about 2 million.

5 The People of Sudan

The more than 40 million people living in Sudan come from many different ethnic and religious backgrounds. About 52 percent of the people are black and 39 percent Arab. Most citizens speak Arabic, and many also speak English and other languages. Some Sudanese live in cities and have office jobs, while others live in mud huts and survive by hunting, fishing, and raising crops. The civil war and the fighting in Darfur caused many people to flee their homes and settle in refuge camps.

Everyday Life

Sudan's major cities and much of its industry is concentrated in the north, where the culture is predominantly Muslim and dominated by Arabs. Modern automobiles and other conveniences are common in the cities. Although some Sudanese, particularly professionals, may wear business

Most of these Sudanese Muslims are wearing traditional gowns (*jalabiyyas*) and white turbans (*emmas*).

dress or western attire, traditionally Muslims living in the country wear long gowns called *jalabiyyas*. They cover their heads in either white or orange skull caps or white turbans called *emmas*. Women traditionally wear a colorful fabric garment, called a *tobe*, which is ten yards long; they wrap these *tobes* around their heads and bodies, obscuring the dresses they wear underneath.

Southern Sudan contains many tribal groups, each speaking different languages. Many of the people living in southern Sudan are farmers and herders. The Dinka are the largest tribe in Sudan, numbering more than 2 million. Other tribes in the south include the Shilluk, Nuer, Nuba, and Azande. The Beja are a group of nomadic camel and goat herders who have been living in Eastern Sudan for 4,000 years. They make up about 6 percent of the population.

Among the Dinka and other nomadic tribes, cows are considered much more than farm animals; they represent wealth and prestige. During the rainy season (April to October), the Dinka live in villages of small homes built from mud and grass, where they cultivate millet. During the dry season, those Dinka who are healthy take their herds to camps by the river.

Religion in Sudan

About 70 percent of Sudan's people follow Islam, a religion first preached by the Prophet Muhammad during the early seventh century. All Muslims are expected to observe five important precepts, also known as the Pillars of Islam. The most important of these is the belief in a single god (Allah) and that Muhammad was his prophet. Each Muslim is also required to pray at different times during each day; give charitable donations to the needy; observe ritual fasting during the holy month of Ramadan; and visit the holy city of Mecca in Saudi Arabia at least once during his or her lifetime, if physically and financially able to do so.

Sharia is a code of behavior based on Islamic scriptures and traditions; it spells out the moral goals of the community and is the basis of laws in some Muslim countries. In northern Sudan, courts look to *Sharia* for guidance when interpreting the law and enforcing justice.

A minority of Sudanese, mostly living in the south, practice either Christianity or traditional African religions. Christianity has a long history in Sudan, dating back to ancient times, but today Christians account for just 5 percent of the population. Most of the tribal Sudanese are animists. They

Quick Facts: The People of Sudan

Population: 41,236,378
Ethnic groups: black 52%, Arab 39%, Beja 6%, foreigners 2%, other 1%
Age structure:
   0–14 years: 42.7%
   15–64 years: 54.9%
   65 years and over: 2.4%
Birth rate: 34.53/1,000 population
Infant mortality rate: 61.05 deaths/1,000 live births
Death rate: 8.97 deaths/1,000 people
Population growth rate: 2.55%
Life expectancy at birth:
   total population: 58.92 years
   male: 57.69 years
   female: 60.21 years

Total fertility rate: 4.72 children born/woman
Religions: Sunni Muslim 70% (in north), indigenous beliefs 25%, Christian 5% (mostly in south and Khartoum)
Languages: Arabic (official), Nubian, Ta Bedawie, diverse dialects of Nilotic, Nilo-Hamitic, Sudanic languages, English
Literacy: 61.1% (2003 est.)

All figures are 2006 estimates unless otherwise indicated.
Source: Adapted from CIA World Factbook, 2007.

believe that all things, including animals and natural features, have spirits, and that the spirits can affect human lives. To win the favor of spirits, religious rituals, including the sacrifice of oxen, are sometimes performed. The spirits of ancestors are also believed to affect the daily lives of tribe members.

Education and Health Care

Primary and secondary education in Sudan is free, although there are few schools in the south and not enough teachers. Few children living in the southern part of the country are able to attend school. Less than half of the total population is able to read and write. Girls are less likely to get an education in Sudan than their brothers. Overall, fewer than 20 percent of Sudanese graduate from high school.

Those who do graduate may attend one of Sudan's nine universities. The oldest and largest of these is the government-run University of Khartoum. With campuses in Khartoum, Khartoum North, and Omdurman, the university has about 17,000 undergraduate and 6,000 postgraduate

A group of Christians sing outside their church in southern Sudan. About 5 percent of Sudan's population are Christians.

students enrolled. However, students cannot attend the university unless they join the Popular Defense Forces, a paramilitary group associated with the National Congress Party. Once enrolled they may pursue degrees in both Sharia and English law as well as agriculture and veterinary sciences, engineering, computer sciences, pharmacy, nursing, architecture, management, and medicine.

Other schools in Sudan include Ahfad University College for Women in Omdurman, the leading women's college in Sudan, and Omdurman Ahlia University, a private school that opened in 1982.

Physicians are in short supply in the country, and doctors must contend with drug shortages and poorly equipped medical facilities. In Sudan there is one doctor for every 6,500 people in the north and one doctor for every 83,000 people in the south. Doctors treat people for diseases rarely found in the developed world—tuberculosis, malaria, snail fever, dysentery, sleeping sickness, black fever, and measles.

Until recently the government of Sudan denied that the virus HIV, which causes the disease AIDS, was a problem in the country. AIDS destroys a person's immune system, making him or her fatally susceptible to normally non-threatening diseases. However, recent reports by UNAIDS, an organization that tracks the spread of the disease throughout the world, indicate that the infection rate in Sudan could be as high as 3 percent of the population.

Sports and Entertainment

The most popular sport in Sudan is soccer. Pick-up games are common among young people, and many Sudanese follow their favorite clubs in an organized

Soccer is among the most popular sports in Sudan. Here, members of the national team (in blue) compete for the ball during a match against Egypt.

league that plays in Khartoum. Sudan also has a national team that competes in the World Cup soccer tournaments and other international events.

Another sport that is popular is wrestling, which is practiced by many tribes. The best Nuba wrestlers compete in ceremonial matches that take place after the tribe's harvest begins. The better the harvest, the more matches are held. Poor harvests mean that there will be no matches at all. It is a great honor to win one of these competitions.

One of Sudan's most famous entertainers is singer Mohamed Wardi, who sings in both Arabic and in his native Nubian dialect. Wardi left the country after Bashir took power and spent 13 years in self-imposed exile in Egypt. However, he still has many fans in Sudan.

Sudan's museums celebrate the country's history. The National Museum is home to archeological artifacts representing every era of Sudanese civilization. An outdoor garden features reconstructed monuments and temples that were rescued from being flooded when the Egyptians built the Aswan Dam. Inside the museum are artifacts from the early Paleolithic period through the coming of Islam. The museum has been open since 1971.

The Khalifa's House Museum is a good place to see artifacts from the Mahdi period in Sudan. The oldest part of the museum was built in 1888 and was occupied by the Mahdi's successor, Khalifa Abdullah ibn Muhammad. The museum has many everyday objects once used by the *khalifa* on display.

A Traditional Meal

The people of Sudan are often glad to share their homes and food with their guests. If one were lucky enough to be invited for dinner, first would come an offer of a refreshing fruit drink called *abre* or *tabrihana*. A sheep might be slaughtered in the visitors' honor.

The guests and family would sit on cushions placed on the floor surrounding a plain, low table. Before eating, everyone would wash their hands at the table using water from a pitcher. After drying their hands with a towel, they would each receive a large cloth to put in their laps to keep their clothing clean. Most foods would be eaten with the right hand.

The first course might be lentil soup or *shorba*, a lamb-based broth fragrant with peanut butter and lemon, served in individual bowls. Next there would be five or six dishes that would be eaten by hand using a flat bread like *kisra*, which resembles a pancake and is made from a grain called **durra**. These dishes could include *maschi* (a tomato dish stuffed with ground beef), *koftah* (ground meatballs), and *salatet zabady bil ajur* (a mixture of plain yogurt, garlic, cucumber, and salt). A spicy condiment called *shata* is also placed on the table for diners to mix with their food.

Meals are usually eaten without a beverage, but after dinner a special coffee called *guhwah* will be served. Sudanese coffee is unlike coffee available in America. Coffee beans are fried over charcoal in a pot called a *jebena*. The fried coffee beans are next ground with cloves and spices and steeped in boiling water. The coffee is strained through a sieve and served in small coffee cups. Non-coffee drinkers might have *kakaday*, hibiscus tea served Sudanese style with plenty of sugar, or *laban*, sweet milk that can be served hot or cold. While the diners drink their steamy beverages, the host may light an incense burner that suffuses the room with a pleasant scent.

The meal is often finished with small slices of peeled fruit, as well as a sweet such as creme caramela, a caramel flavored pudding, or *zabadi*, a honey sweetened yogurt.

According to UN statistics, most residents of Sudan live in rural villages. Just 41 percent of the population lives in urban areas. (Opposite) This aerial view of Khartoum, Sudan's largest city, shows the al-Farouq mosque. (Right) UN peacekeepers patrol a street in Juba, the capital of southern Sudan.

6 Sudanese Communities

All of the most populous cities (those with more than 500,000 people) in Sudan are located in the northern part of the country. The largest city in southern Sudan is Juba, with an estimated 2007 population of about 250,000. Khartoum, Khartoum North (Bahri), and Omdurman make up Sudan's biggest metropolis, together housing an estimated 6.3 million people. Port Sudan, while not home to as many people, is indispensable to Sudan's economy as it is the only seaport.

Khartoum

The best-known city in Sudan is Khartoum, which in Arabic means "elephant trunk," a shape the city resembles from above. The city is located at the spot where the Blue Nile and White Nile come together. It is connected to its nearby

61

sister cities of Khartoum North and Omdurman by bridges. As the capital of Sudan, Khartoum is home to embassies and other government-related offices. Most of the country's businesses are headquartered there, along with many of the country's doctors and professionals.

Despite being the country's capital, Khartoum is not a big tourist destination. It has only 11 hotels. Only recently has the city's telephone system become reliable. There is one television station in the entire country and few radio stations. From midnight to 5 A.M. in Khartoum, people on the streets are subject to questioning by the police. Foreigners may be asked to show their passports. Furthermore, no photographs can be taken within the city without a permit, and photographs of military areas, bridges, public utilities, broadcasting stations, and street people are never allowed.

Visitors to North Khartoum will find dockyards, meat packing plants, textile weaving enterprises, rubber plants, concrete manufacturing, and shoe manufacturing. North Khartoum also contains some of the most expensive houses in the area. In nearby Omdurman, mud-walled houses are typical abodes for city workers.

A sad legacy of Sudan's civil war can be seen on the streets of Khartoum, where thousands of homeless orphans must fend for themselves. More than a million Sudanese still live in refugee camps near the city.

Omdurman

About 3 million people live in Omdurman, a city that is not quite as modern as Khartoum. Roads in Omdurman are unpaved, and there is no commercial center. However, the city does have the largest marketplace in Sudan, the

Souk el-Kebir. For 1,800 years peddlers and craftsman have lined its narrow streets, jostling for customers. At the *souk* one can purchase food, handmade crafts and jewelry, and many other items. Located near the *souk* is a more specialized marketplace—Omdurman's camel market (the Mowelih).

Sudanese dervishes perform a ritual outside the Hamad al-Nile shrine in Omdurman. The dervishes are Sufi Muslims who believe that they can experience Allah (God) through rituals and dancing.

Omdurman is also home to the Mahdi's tomb and to the Khalifa's House Museum. The original Mahdi's tomb was destroyed when the British recaptured the city, but because of the tomb's historical significance it was rebuilt in 1947.

Omdurman is famous for its *dervishes*, religious Muslims who dance themselves into a frenzy every Friday. Dressed in white from their turbans to their jalabiyyas, these men gather in western Omdurman in front of the tomb of Sheikh Hamad al-Nile, a 19th century holy man who was believed to be able to perform miracles. The dervishes form a circle and, to the beat of drums and chants, whirl around in dizzying fashion to remove themselves from everyday life and become closer to God.

Port Sudan

Port Sudan, the country's only seaport, is located on the Red Sea about 800 miles (1,287 km) northeast of Khartoum. It is through Port Sudan that the Sudanese trade their goods with the rest of the world. The British established the city in 1905; today it is home to about a million people, including refugees from Chad, Uganda, Eritrea, and Ethiopia. Pilgrims on the way to Mecca in Saudi Arabia often pass through the city.

While Port Sudan is not the thriving terminal it once was, there are signs that its fortunes may be improving. An international chain recently built a luxury hotel in the city. Also encouraging was the news that Ethiopia, which has no seaport of its own, has agreed to use Port Sudan for its shipping needs. Most importantly, a pipeline completed in 1999 brings oil from Sudan's oil fields to tankers anchored at the port.

Juba

Juba is the capital of Southern Sudan, as well as of the Sudanese state of Central Equatoria. It is located on the White Nile River and is an important river port. Although Juba is the largest city in the region, it is primarily made up of mud huts and derelict buildings. Electrical service and clean water are often unavailable to the city's residents.

Juba was once a transportation center, with highways to neighboring countries like Kenya, Uganda, and the Democratic Republic of the Congo. However, during the Second Sudanese Civil War a great deal of fighting occurred around the city and the road network was essentially destroyed. The roads are only now being repaired.

A Calendar of Sudanese Festivals

Muslim Holidays

The dates of Muslim holidays, such as **Ramadan**, are determined using a lunar calendar that is shorter than the 365-day solar year used in Western countries. This means that each year, Muslim holidays are held 10 or 11 days earlier than the year before. Thus, any Muslim holiday could be celebrated during any month in the Western calendar.

The **Muslim New Year** marks the beginning of the Islamic month known as Muharram.

Mawlid an-Nabi, the commemoration of the birthday of the Prophet Mohammed, is celebrated by prayer and often a procession to the local mosque. Families gather for feasts, often featuring the foods that were reportedly the favorites of Mohammed: dates, grapes, almonds, and honey. This holiday occurs on the 12th day of the month Rabi'-ul-Awwal.

The month of Ramadan is the holiest season of the year for Muslims. During Ramadan, Muslims are supposed to fast during the day, pray, and perform good deeds. At the end of Ramadan comes **Eid al-Fitr**, a feast and celebration lasting three days. This is a a joyous holiday in which Muslims visit family and friends, give gifts, and enjoy meals.

Eid al-Adha is celebrated on the 10th day of the Islamic month of Dhul Hijja. It observes the Prophet Abraham's willingness to sacrifice his son for God. It also marks the end of the *Hajj*, a ritual pilgrimage that all Muslims are expected to make to Mecca at least once during their lifetimes, if they are physically and financially able to do so.

January

Sudan has few national holidays. On January 1, the Sudanese people celebrate their liberation from the Egyptian and British Condominium Government on **Independence Day**. Soldiers parade through the streets of Khartoum to mark the occasion.

On January 7, members of the Coptic Christian Church celebrate **Christmas**, the birth of Jesus Christ. The Coptic Church is an ancient sect that once flourished in the region.

March

Unity Day, celebrated on March 27, commemorates the signing of the Addis Ababa agreement in 1972. The agreement ended the civil war for a time and gave hope that peace would last. It did not.

April

Christians celebrate the season of **Lent**, a time of prayer and self-sacrifice, between February and April; the dates of the season vary from year to year. Lent lasts for 40 days. The last week of Lent is known as Passion Week, and recognizes the arrival of Jesus in Jerusalem on **Palm Sunday**; the **Last Supper** on Holy Thursday; and the cruci-

A Calendar of Sudanese Festivals

fixion on **Good Friday**. These are followed by **Easter Sunday**, when Christians celebrate the resurrection of Jesus. Easter always falls between March 22 and April 25.

June

Revolution Day, observed on June 30, commemorates the military coup that brought Omar al-Bashir to power in 1989.

December

Christians who do not follow the Coptic tradition celebrate **Christmas** on December 25.

Recipes

Maschi (Stuffed Tomato with Chopped Beef)

2 lbs. chopped beef
1 tsp. salt
1/2 tsp. pepper
1 tsp. garlic powder (or 2 cloves mashed)
4 tbs. chopped fresh dill (or 1 tsp. dried dill)
2 tbs. salad oil
1 cup cooked rice
8 large tomatoes
2 tbs. butter
2 tbs. oil

Sauce:
2 6 oz. cans tomato paste
2 6 oz. cans water
1/2 tsp. salt
1 tsp. cinnamon
1 tsp. garlic powder
green olives

Directions:
1. Sauté beef with salt, pepper, garlic powder, dill, and oil until meat browns. Add cooked rice.
2. Cut and open a slit in each tomato. Scoop out the inside of the tomato. Fill tomato with beef mixture and close slit.
3. Melt butter and oil in a skillet and sauté tomatoes until dark red. Remove tomatoes and place in a heavy saucepan.
4. Combine tomato paste, water, salt, cinnamon, and garlic powder and pour over tomatoes. Simmer over low heat for 10 to 15 minutes. Garnish with green olive slices.

Sudani Rice

3 cups rice
1 tbs. butter or oil
1 tsp. salt
pinch of turmeric (optional)
pinch of coriander (optional)
pinch of cardamom (optional)

Directions:
1. In pot, fry rice in butter or oil for 1 to 2 minutes. Pour water into pot until covering rice by an inch.
2. Add salt and turmeric or coriander or cardamom. Cover and cook until water evaporated.

68

Shorba

3 lbs. lamb bones
2 quarts water
2 tsp. salt
1/2 lb. whole onions, peeled
1/2 lb. carrots, peeled and cut in chunks
1/2 lb. cabbage, cut in small wedges
1/2 lb. string beans, trimmed
3 cloves garlic, chopped finely
4 tbs. peanut butter thinned with juice of 1 lemon

Directions:

1. Simmer lamb bones in water with salt for one hour. Add onions, carrots, cabbage, string beans, and garlic. Simmer for 1 hour until vegetables are thoroughly cooked.
2. Remove lamb bones and put the mixture through a sieve or food mill. Mix peanut butter with the juice of one lemon. Add peanut butter to soup puree. Season with salt and pepper.

Glossary

condominium—a system under which a territory is ruled by two or more nations, which share equal rights to the land and resources. Such forms of rule are rare because they rely on the cooperation of multiple governments.

coup—the sudden overthrow of a government, especially by the military.

dervish—a follower of Sufism, or Islamic mysticism, whose style of worship includes using physical movement (such as dancing) to enter a trancelike state.

durra—a grain grown for food and animal feed in tropical or arid areas.

fundamentalist—someone who participates in a religious movement based on a literal interpretation of religious doctrine and strict adherence to that doctrine.

gross domestic product—the value of all goods and services produced in a country during a one-year period.

haboob—a violent dust storm that occurs in Sudan. These storms can blot out the sun, and people are advised to take shelter until they pass.

indigenous—native to a particular region.

inflation—an increase in the supply of money and credit relative to available goods and services, resulting in a continuing rise in the general price level.

Islamist—radical, militant, or extremist Muslim beliefs.

judicial review—the doctrine that gives courts the authority to determine whether laws are unconstitutional and have them nullified.

junta—a group that takes control of a country following a coup.

martial law—law administered by military forces during a period of war, unrest, or another emergency during which the civilian government may be unable to maintain order.

millet—a fast-growing cereal plant used for food in Africa.

savanna—a flat grassland in a tropical or subtropical region.

sorghum—a tall cereal grass cultivated in tropical areas as a grain crop and for animal feed.

steppe—an area of flat, treeless land similar to a prairie, but with short grasses.

talisman—an object that is believed to have magical powers or serve a religious purpose.

Project and Report Ideas

Map the Conflict

Draw a map of Sudan and mark the individual states. Color the southern states that have recently formed their own government a different color from the North. Include major topographical features like mountain ranges and the Nile River.

Study the Nile River

Draw a map which shows the Blue and White Nile rivers and where they meet. Research the sources of both rivers and explain how their water flows are different. How do these differences affect the Nile in Egypt?

Sides of the War

Civil war was a major component of Sudan's history. Research the culture of the North and the culture of the South. What do they believe? How are they different? How did the civil war start? How did it come to an end?

Learn through Cooking

Refer to the section on a traditional meal in Chapter 5 and the included recipes. Cook a dish and present it to the class. Explain how meals are served and how Islam influences what foods are eaten.

Project and Report Ideas

Ancient Sudan

At one time, the culture of Kush was much like that of Egypt. Research the kingdom of Kush and find out how they were similar to the Egyptians. Did they use hieroglyphics? Did they build pyramids?

Write a Biography

Chose a name from the following list of important figures from Sudan's history. Do research at the library or on the Internet to find out about this person, and write a one-page biography:

- Muhammad Ali
- Muhammad Ahmed (the Mahdi)
- Abdullah ibn Muhammad
- Charles Gordon
- Horatio Herbert Kitchener
- Ibrahim Abbud
- Sirr al-Khatim al-Khalifa
- Jaafar al-Nimeri
- Joseph Lagu
- Sadiq al-Mahdi
- Hassan al-Turabi
- Omar Hassan al-Bashir
- John Garang

Chronology

ca. 2000 B.C.:	The early civilization of Kush trades with Egypt.
ca. 1500:	Kush becomes a province of Egypt under the rule of Pharaoh Ahmose I.
750:	The Kushite king Kashta conquers portions of Egypt.
ca. 600:	Merotic civilization begins to rise along the Nile.
24:	Angered by Merotic incursions into Roman-controlled Egypt, Roman legions invade Meroe and bring the region under imperial control.
ca. A.D. 570:	Muhammad, whose teaching will become the basis of Islam, is born; three Nubian kingdoms in the Sudan region (Nobatia, Muqurra, and Alwa) are converted to Christianity.
652:	Nubians resist the advance of Islam and sign a peace agreement.
1276:	The Mamluk rulers of Egypt gain power over Sudan.
1517:	The Ottoman Turks absorb Egypt and Sudan into their empire.
1820:	The Egyptian warlord Muhammad Ali sends a force to invade Sudan. The region soon comes under Egypt's control.
1869:	The Suez Canal opens.
1882:	Great Britain becomes involved in Egyptian and Sudanese affairs.
1883:	The Mahdi declares *jihad* against the foreign rule of the Sudan.
1898:	The forces of the *khalifa* are defeated by British troops under Lord Kitchener.
1899:	The condominium period of joint rule by Great Britain and Egypt begins.
1955:	The First Sudanese Civil War begins, pitting rebels from southern Sudan against the incoming government in Khartoum.
1956:	Sudan becomes an independent country.
1964:	Sudanese students, civil servants, and trade unionists protest against the Abbud government. Riots break out in Khartoum and other cities.
1965:	New elections are held, and a coalition government led by Muhammad Ahmed Mahjub is elected.

Chronology

1966: Mahjub is forced to step down, and Sadiq al-Mahdi takes power.

1967: Mahdi coalition government collapses, and Mahjub returns to power as prime minister.

1969: Jaafar al-Nimeri takes over the government.

1972: Southern Sudan becomes autonomous under the Addis Ababa agreement, and much of the fighting ends.

1973: Sudan's first constitution is adopted.

1983: President Nimeri declares Sharia to be the law of Sudan, and the civil war resumes after a 10-year break.

1985: Coup against Nimeri leaves military government in charge.

1986: Sadiq al-Mahdi forms coalition government.

1989: A military coup planned by Hassan al-Turabi, leader of the National Islamic Front, is carried out by General Omar al-Bashir; Bashir imposes martial law in the country.

1993: Bashir is elected president of Sudan.

1998: The United States destroys a pharmaceutical factory suspected of making chemical weapons in Khartoum.

2000: Bashir is reelected to a second five-year term with 86 percent of the vote in an election widely condemned as rigged.

2003: Armed conflict breaks out in the Darfur region of western Sudan.

2005: A peace agreement is signed allowing an elected government for the South, which may choose to secede in the future.

2006: Sudan refuses to allow UN peacekeeping troops to enter the country and assist in ending the Darfur conflict.

2007: The United Nations estimates that more than 400,000 people have been killed in Darfur.

Further Reading/Internet Resources

Daley, M. W., and P. M. Holt. *A History of the Sudan from the Coming of Islam to the Present Day*. Boston: Addison-Wesley, 2000.

Metz, Helen Chapin, ed. *Sudan: A Country Study*. Washington, D.C.: Library of Congress, 1992.

Petterson, Donald. *Inside Sudan: Political Islam, Conflict, and Catastrophe*. Boulder, Colo.: Westview Press, 1999.

Snyder, Gail. *Sudan*. Philadelphia: Mason Crest, 2003.

Travel Information

http://lonelyplanet.com/destinations/africa/sudan/
http://www.worldtravelguide.net/country/country_guide.ehtml?o=266

History and Geography

http://www.stockton.edu/~gilmorew/consorti/1iafric.htm
http://www.sudan.net/government/constitution/english.html
http://www.zum.de/whkmla/region/northafrica/xsudan.html

Economic and Political Information

http://www.sudanembassy.org

Culture and Festivals

http://www.sudan.net
http://sudanartists.org
http://www.m-huether.de/sudan/sudart/

Embassy of the Republic of Sudan
2210 Massachusetts Ave. NW
Washington, DC 20008
Tel: (202) 338-8565
Fax: (202) 667-2406
Email: info@sudanembassy.org

U.S. Department of State (travel advisories)
2201 C St. NW
Washington, DC 20520
Phone: (202) 647-5225
Fax: (202) 647-3000
Website: http://travel.state.gov

Index

Numbers in ***bold italic*** refer to captions.

Contributors/Picture Credits

Professor Robert I. Rotberg is Director of the Program on Intrastate Conflict and Conflict Resolution at the Kennedy School, Harvard University, and President of the World Peace Foundation. He is the author of a number of books and articles on Africa, including *A Political History of Tropical Africa* and *Ending Autocracy, Enabling Democracy: The Tribulations of Southern Africa.*

Dorothy Kavanaugh is a freelance writer who lives near Philadelphia. She holds a bachelor's degree in elementary education from Bryn Mawr College. Books she has written for young adults include *Religions of Africa* (Mason Crest, 2007.)